To Isaac,

from Grandad Boyd

October, 2002.

Bible Stories for Bedtime

this book belongs to: _____

CHRISTIAN FOCUS

Note to Parents
(or any adult reading this book to a young child)

Encourage your child to start the good habit of Bible reading and prayer at bedtime. These stories are short and just give a taste of the wonderful treasure store that we have in the Bible. The prayers after each story are merely suggestions - you may have to alter the details to fit in with your child's experience.

©1999 Christian Focus
ISBN 1-85792-467-3

Published by Christian Focus Publications Ltd,
Geanies House, Fearn, Tain, Ross-shire
IV20 1TW, Scotland, Great Britain

Text by Carine Mackenzie
Illustrations by Fred Apps

Printed in Singapore

Contents

Noah's Big Test

Noah and his wife loved God very much. Sadly, all the other people in the world did not love God and went their own way. God was not pleased with them.

God told Noah to build a large boat, made of wood. It would have to be big enough to fit Noah, his wife, his three sons and two of every kind of animal. Noah thought this was strange, but he trusted God and obeyed him. It was just as well that he did!

When God sent the flood, everyone and everything was destroyed. Noah and his family were safely tucked away inside the boat. They weren't alone. Each type of animal that God had made was safely shut up inside the boat with them.

PRAYER: Thank you Lord for giving me your Word, the Bible.
Help me to obey what you tell me to do.

The Long Journey

Abraham and his wife Sarah lived in a city called Ur. They were quite settled there, until one day, when God spoke to them. 'Leave your home and travel to another land. I will show you where to go.'

Abraham trusted that God would show him the way, and so they set out on their long journey.

The journey was not an easy one. They had all sorts of problems. At last when they reached the land of Canaan God said to Abraham.
'Look at all this land. It will belong to your children.'

Abraham believed God and trusted and worshipped him.

PRAYER: Lord, please keep me safe as I go out, and when I play with my friends.

A Special Promise

God had given Abraham and Sarah a promise that they would have a son. Years passed by and both of them began to grow old. There was still no baby.

When God's messengers came to tell Abraham and Sarah that they would soon have a baby, Sarah laughed in amazement. She had doubted God's promise. But God was faithful to his word and Sarah did have a son. Abraham called him Isaac.

Nothing is too hard for God. Baby Isaac was born when his father was 100 years old. His mother was 90 years old. Abraham had believed in God's promise and he was not disappointed!

PRAYER: Thank you Lord for looking after me when I was a baby. Thank you for giving my family to care for me.

Abraham Trusts God

One day God said to Abraham, 'Take your son Isaac whom you love so much, to Mount Moriah. Sacrifice him as an offering to me.'

Abraham trusted God. He believed all things were possible with God. God could even raise Isaac from the dead! He obeyed God faithfully. He took Isaac up the mountain and prepared to sacrifice him on the altar. But just as he raised the knife, the angel of the Lord called out to Abraham and told him not to harm the boy. Abraham looked up and saw a ram caught by its horns in a bush. God had provided the ram for the sacrifice.

How joyfully Abraham and Isaac would have come down the hill. Abraham's faith in God had been rewarded.

PRAYER: Thank you Father for sending your son Jesus into the world.
Thank you that he died to take away all my sin.
Help me to be a follower of Jesus.

The River Baby

Amram and Jochabed lived in Egypt. They were Hebrews. The Egyptian ruler, called Pharaoh was cruel to the Hebrew people and ordered all baby boys to be killed.

When baby Moses was born, his parents decided to hide him in the house. As he grew bigger and bigger he began to get noisier and noisier. They had to do something - quickly!

His mother made a little basket out of bulrushes and made sure that it was waterproof. Baby Moses was safely tucked up inside and the basket was placed in the River.

Amram and Jochabed trusted that God would take care of their little baby boy. God had a special plan for Moses and he did look after him.

PRAYER: Please keep me safe as I sleep in bed tonight.
Take care of me as you took care of Moses long ago.

Escape from Egypt

God's people were upset. The Pharaoh of Egypt had treated them badly. God heard the cry of his people and sent Moses to help them.

Moses stood up to Pharaoh. He knew God was on his side. With God's help, Moses led the people out of Egypt.

The soldiers chased after Moses and the people, right to the edge of the Red Sea. God told Moses to stretch out his hand over the sea. The waters parted and the people walked across on dry land.

Moses had trusted in his God. Moses saw God's great power.

PRAYER: Thank you for my teachers.
Help me to remember what I learn about you.

Hannah prays for a son

Hannah longed to have a baby of her own. One day when she was in the Temple of the Lord she prayed earnestly to God. She made a promise to God. 'If you will give me a baby boy,' she said, 'I will give him back to work for the Lord God all his life.'

Hannah believed that God would answer her prayer. She went back home content. Hannah's prayer was answered. Soon she and her husband Elkanah did have a baby boy. She called his name Samuel which means, 'Asked of God.'

Hannah did not forget her promise to God. When Samuel was old enough she brought him to the temple in Shiloh to work there with Eli the priest. He worked for the Lord God there.

PRAYER: Thank you for my church, which is your house.
Help me to worship you there.
Thank you that I can worship you anywhere.

Samuel works in the temple

Samuel worked hard in the temple helping Eli with all sorts of tasks. Eli was growing old and he was very pleased to have young Samuel to assist him.

Hannah and Elkanah came to Shiloh every year for the special service in the temple. Hannah brought a new coat for Samuel each time she came. She had made it herself. God was pleased with Samuel and the way he worshipped and served him. Everybody who knew Samuel liked him.

Samuel trusted God in everything that he did, even in the ordinary everyday activities of work in the Temple.

Prayer: Thank you for taking care of me each day.
Thank you for the lovely clothes I have to wear.

Samuel listens to God

One evening Samuel lay down on his bed ready to go to sleep. He heard a voice calling him by name. He hurried through to Eli thinking he had called. But he hadn't called.

This happened a second time. The third time Samuel ran through to the old man, Eli gave him some advice. When you hear the voice calling you again reply, 'Speak, Lord, for your servant is listening.'

The voice did call Samuel again and he replied, 'Speak, Lord, for your servant is listening.' God spoke to Samuel and told him what he was going to do to Eli's sons, who disobeyed God. Samuel lay in bed till the morning thinking about what God had told him.

Samuel grew up to be prophet of God - speaking God's words to the people. God guided him all his life.

PRAYER: Thank you for older people who love me - especially my grandparents. Help me to listen to their wise advice.

Chosen to be king

Samuel was told by God to go to Jesse's house. One of Jesse's sons was God's choice for the next king. It was Samuel's job to find him.

One by one Jesse's handsome sons were brought to Samuel. 'No, he is not the right one. Have you any other sons?' Samuel asked.

'Yes,' replied Jesse, 'there is David, the youngest. He is out in the fields looking after the sheep.'
'Bring him immediately.'

David came to meet Samuel. 'This is the one,' God told him. 'Anoint him as king.'

Samuel poured oil on David's head to show that he had been chosen by God to be king one day.

PRAYER: Thank you Lord for my family - for my brothers and sisters and cousins.
Help me to be a loving friend to them.

David talks to the king

David's brother's were soldiers in the army of King Saul. They were fighting against the powerful Philistine army.

David was sent one day by his father to see how the brothers were getting on and to take a gift of some cheeses to their captain.

While he was there the big giant Goliath who was the champion soldier of the Philistine army, shouted defiantly to the men of Saul's army. Everybody was afraid.

David wanted to know more. Why would no one fight this evil man? The king sent for him. 'I will go and fight this giant,' said David.
'You are just a boy,' replied Saul.
'I have fought a lion and a bear with the help of God,' replied David. 'The same God can help me to fight Goliath.'
'Go ahead,' said Saul. 'The Lord be with you.'

PRAYER: Dear God, please help me to fight against evil and sin in my life.

Help me to be brave like David was.

The Big Fight

David dressed in his simple shepherd's clothes, and with his staff in his hand, went down to the stream. He picked out five smooth stones and put them in his shepherd's bag.

When Goliath saw the young boy coming towards him with his shepherd's sling, he was very angry. He shouted insults at David. David was brave. He was trusting in God.

'You have come to fight with big weapons,' he told Goliath, 'but I fight in the name of the Lord God. He will help me to win.'

David reached into his bag, took out a stone, slung a shot and struck Goliath right in the middle of his forehead. He fell down dead. God had helped David defeat his enemy. All the Philistine soldiers ran away when they realised that their champion was dead.

PRAYER: Lord God, help me to trust you when I face a difficult time.
I need you always.

Fed by the ravens

Elijah was a good man. He was not afraid to speak God's word to anybody, even the king.

God told Elijah to warn King Ahab that there would be no rain or dew on the land for some years. Ahab was angry because Elijah had given him this bad news.

God told Elijah 'Go east across the river Jordan and hide beside the brook Cherith'. Elijah drank water from the brook. Every morning and evening ravens brought bread and meat for him to eat. God took care of Elijah in this lonely place and supplied all his needs.

God takes care of us too. He gives us many good gifts. All our food and drink are gifts from God. We should remember to say thank you.

Prayer: Thank you Lord for all the food and drink I had today.
Every meal and snack is provided by you. Help me not to forget that.

God looks after the poor

Elijah moved on to the city of Zarephath.
'There is a widow there who will give you some food,' God told him.
Elijah met the woman, gathering up sticks, at the city gate.

'Bring me a drink of water and a piece of bread,' he asked her.
'I have hardly any food left,' she said, 'I'm about to cook one last meal for myself and my son before we die of starvation.'

'Make a little cake for me first,' Elijah persuaded her. 'Your barrel of meal and your jug of oil will last as long as this drought lasts.'

The woman did as Elijah asked and was amazed to find that the meal and oil lasted for as long as it was needed.

Prayer: Lord help me to be kind and generous with my toys and treats. Help me to share what I have with my friends.

God can be trusted

One day the widow who had helped Elijah came to him in great distress. Her only son had become ill. He grew worse and worse and eventually died. Could Elijah do anything to help? Elijah carried the boy up to the bed in his room. He stretched himself out on top of the boy's body three times and prayed that the Lord would bring him back to life.

God heard Elijah's prayers. The boy's life returned to him. Elijah picked him up and carried him downstairs to his mother.

The woman was overjoyed. 'Now I know that you are a man of God. The word of God that you speak is the truth.'

The woman had helped Elijah when he was in need. Elijah now helped the woman in her time of trouble. God used both of these people to carry out his purposes.

Prayer: Thank you for making me better when I have been ill.
Thank you for the doctors and nurses who work to help sick people.

Daniel prays to God

Daniel was a fine young man who had been taken to live in the land of Babylon. Even in this strange land he did not forget the Lord God. He prayed to him three times a day. He thanked God for his goodness and asked him for his help. The king thought very highly of Daniel and gave him an important position. Some of the other officials were jealous of Daniel and planned to harm him.

They persuaded the king to pass a law ordering people to pray only to the king himself. The king was very flattered. But of course Daniel wouldn't pray to the king! He would only pray to the Lord God - the only true God.

Even when he was threatened with punishment, Daniel would not stop praying to God. He loved and trusted him.

Prayer: Lord thank you for listening to me when I pray to you.
Help me to remember to pray often.

Safe in the lions' den

The nasty officials had planned a terrible punishment for Daniel. He was thrown into a den of lions. A big stone was placed over the entrance to the den. There was no way out. The king was miserable. How he wished that he had not allowed such a law to be passed. 'Perhaps Daniel's God will help him,' he thought.

The next morning the king hurried to the den. He called out to Daniel and to his great joy Daniel shouted back. 'My God sent his angels to shut the lions' mouths. They have not hurt me at all.'

Daniel was lifted out of the lions' den without a scratch. He had trusted in God and God had kept him safe in a very dangerous place.

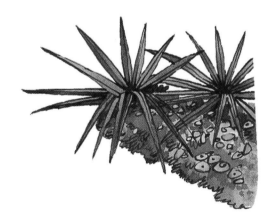

Prayer: Lord I praise and thank you for your power and love.
You saved Daniel. I ask you to save me from the power of sin.

God is the same today

We read in the Bible of many men and women who loved and trusted God in so many situations. We can learn from them and ask God to help us to love and trust him too.

We can trust God in times of danger like Noah and Daniel did. We should trust God in our day to day activities, just like young Samuel.

Prayer: Thank you God that you are the same yesterday today and forever. You never change. I can always trust and rely on you.
Help me to learn from people like Noah and Daniel who loved and trusted you.

God will help you

Do we remember like Elijah that it is God who provides us with our food, even if we do buy it in the supermarket?

When we travel like Abraham and Sarah we should ask God to keep us safe. Just as God helped David to fight against the big frightening giant Goliath, so God will help us to fight against Satan the evil one.

Prayer: Lord God, you look after me so well. Thank you for your love and care.
Teach me how to pray to you and help me to love you more every day.
You give me so many good things. You are wonderful.

God speaks to us

God wants us to speak to him in prayer asking for his blessing and forgiveness.

God's word is important for us too. It can guide us in difficult times, it can comfort us when we are sad. It teaches us to do God's will.

In it we learn about the Lord Jesus Christ and how he died to save us from our sins.

Prayer: Thank you for your word the Bible. Thank you for its teaching and comfort and guidance. I pray for your blessing on my life and ask you to forgive my sins through the Lord Jesus who died on the cross to save his followers.